French Short Stories for Beginners Book 3

Over 100 Dialogues and Daily Used Phrases to Learn French in Your Car. Have Fun & Grow Your Vocabulary, with Crazy Effective Language Learning Lessons

www.LearnLikeNatives.com

www.LearnLikeNatives.com

© Copyright 2020
By Learn Like A Native

ALL RIGHTS RESERVED

No part of this book may be reproduced, stored in a retrieval system, or transmitted in any form or by any means, without the prior written permission of the publisher.

www.LearnLikeNatives.com

TABLE OF CONTENT

INTRODUCTION	5
CHAPTER 1 The Car / emotions	17
Translation of the Story	35
The Car	35
CHAPTER 2 Going to A Meeting / telling time	47
Translation of the Story	64
Going to A Meeting	64
CHAPTER 3 Lunch with The Queen / to be, to have + food	75
Translation of the Story	93
Lunch With The Queen	93
CONCLUSION	105
About the Author	111

www.LearnLikeNatives.com

www.LearnLikeNatives.com

INTRODUCTION

Before we dive into some French, I want to congratulate you, whether you're just beginning, continuing, or resuming your language learning journey. Here at Learn Like a Native, we understand the determination it takes to pick up a new language and after reading this book, you'll be another step closer to achieving your language goals. As a thank you for learning with us, we are giving you free access to our 'Speak Like a Native' eBook. It's packed full of practical advice and insider tips on how to make language learning quick, easy, and most importantly, enjoyable. Head over to LearnLikeNatives.com to access your free guide and peruse our huge selection of language learning resources.

www.LearnLikeNatives.com

Learning a new language is a bit like cooking—you need several different ingredients and the right technique, but the end result is sure to be delicious. We created this book of short stories for learning French because language is alive. Language is about the senses—hearing, tasting the words on your tongue, and touching another culture up close. Learning a language in a classroom is a fine place to start, but it's not a complete introduction to a language.

In this book, you'll find a language come to life. These short stories are miniature immersions into the French language, at a level that is perfect for beginners. This book is not a lecture on grammar. It's not an endless vocabulary list. This book is the closest you can come to a language immersion without leaving the country. In the stories within, you will see people speaking to each other, going through daily life situations, and using the most common, helpful words and phrases in language.

www.LearnLikeNatives.com

You are holding the key to bringing your French studies to life.

Made for Beginners

We made this book with beginners in mind. You'll find that the language is simple, but not boring. Most of the book is in the present tense, so you will be able to focus on dialogues, root verbs, and understand and find patterns in subject-verb agreement.

This is not "just" a translated book. While reading novels and short stories translated into French is a wonderful thing, beginners (and even novices) often run into difficulty. Literary licenses and complex sentence structure can make reading in your second language truly difficult—not to mention BORING. That's why French Short Stories for Beginners is the perfect book to pick up. The stories are simple, but not infantile. They were not written for children, but the language is simple so that beginners can pick it up.

The Benefits of Learning a Second Language

If you have picked up this book, it's likely that you are already aware of the many benefits of learning a second language. Besides just being fun, knowing more than one language opens up a whole new world to you. You will be able to communicate with a much larger chunk of the world. Opportunities in the workforce will open up, and maybe even your day-to-day work will be improved. Improved communication can also help you expand your business. And from a neurological perspective, learning a second language is like taking your daily vitamins and eating well, for your brain!

www.LearnLikeNatives.com

How To Use The Book

The chapters of this book all follow the same structure:

- A short story with several dialogs
- A summary in French
- A list of important words and phrases and their English translation
- Questions to test your understanding
- Answers to check if you were right
- The English translation of the story to clear every doubt

You may use this book however is comfortable for you, but we have a few recommendations for getting the most out of the experience. Try these tips and if they work for you, you can use them on every chapter throughout the book.

1) Start by reading the story all the way through. Don't stop or get hung up on any particular words or phrases. See how much of the plot you can understand in this way. We think you'll get a lot more of it than you may expect, but it is completely normal not to understand everything in the story. You are learning a new language, and that takes time.

2) Read the summary in French. See if it matches what you have understood of the plot.

3) Read the story through again, slower this time. See if you can pick up the meaning of any words or phrases you don't understand by using context clues and the information from the summary.

4) Test yourself! Try to answer the five comprehension questions that come at the end of each story. Write your answers

down, and then check them against the answer key. How did you do? If you didn't get them all, no worries!

5) Look over the vocabulary list that accompanies the chapter. Are any of these the words you did not understand? Did you already know the meaning of some of them from your reading?

6) Now go through the story once more. Pay attention this time to the words and phrases you haven't understand. If you'd like, take the time to look them up to expand your meaning of the story. Every time you read over the story, you'll understand more and more.

7) Move on to the next chapter when you are ready.

www.LearnLikeNatives.com

Read and Listen

The audio version is the best way to experience this book, as you will hear a native French speaker tell you each story. You will become accustomed to their accent as you listen along, a huge plus for when you want to apply your new language skills in the real world.

If this has ignited your language learning passion and you are keen to find out what other resources are available, go to LearnLikeNatives.com, where you can access our vast range of free learning materials. Don't know where to begin? An excellent place to start is our 'Speak Like a Native' free eBook, full of practical advice and insider tips on how to make language learning quick, easy, and most importantly, enjoyable.

www.LearnLikeNatives.com

And remember, small steps add up to great advancements! No moment is better to begin learning than the present.

www.LearnLikeNatives.com

FREE BOOK!

Get the *FREE BOOK* that reveals the secrets path to learn any language fast, and without leaving your country.

Discover:

- The **language 5 golden rules** to master languages at will

- Proven **mind training techniques** to revolutionize your learning

- A complete step-by-step guide to **conquering any language**

www.LearnLikeNatives.com

www.LearnLikeNatives.com

www.LearnLikeNatives.com

CHAPTER 1
The Car / emotions

HISTOIRE

Quentin **s'intéresse** aux voitures. Il regarde des photos de voitures. Il lit des choses sur les voitures toute la nuit, toutes les nuits. Quand il **s'ennuie**, il parcourt Instagram. Les comptes qu'il suit sont dédiés aux voitures.

La petite amie de Quentin est Rashel. Rashel est **amusée** par l'obsession de Quentin. Les voitures ne l'intéressent pas.

Quentin a une voiture. Quentin conduit une Honda Accord 2000. Sa voiture est verte. Quentin est **gêné** par sa voiture. Il veut une voiture cool. Il veut une voiture pour faire le tour de la ville avec Rashel. Il rêve de belles voitures, de voitures chères. Il veut une grande voiture. Les petites voitures sont ennuyeuses.

Ces derniers temps, Quentin regarde son téléphone tout le temps. Quand Rashel le regarde, Quentin le cache.

« Quentin, pourquoi me caches-tu le téléphone? demande Rashel.

- Il n'y a pas de raison, dit Quentin.

- Ce n'est pas vrai! dit Rashel.

- Je te le promets! dit Quentin.

- Alors laisse-moi voir l'écran, dit Rashel.

- Ce n'est rien, dit Quentin. Oublie cela. »

Rashel est méfiante. Quentin cache quelque chose.

Un soir, Rashel fait le dîner. Le téléphone de Quentin sonne. Elle ne connaît pas le numéro. Quentin répond au téléphone.

« Bonjour ? Oh. Je vous appellerai plus tard », dit Quentin. Il raccroche.

« Qui est-ce ? dit Rashel.

- Personne, dit Quentin.

- Est-ce une fille? demande Rashel. Elle est **jalouse**.

- Non, ce n'est pas le cas, dit Quentin.

- Alors qui est-ce ? demande Rashel.

- Personne, dit Quentin.

- Pourquoi ne me le dis-tu pas ? » demande Rashel.

Il est tellement **en colère**, Quentin sort de la maison. Il laisse le plat sur la table. Il fait froid. Rashel est **triste**. Le dîner est un gâchis. Rashel appelle son ami. Ils parlent du dîner. L'ami de Rashel pense que Quentin est avec une autre fille. Rashel n'en est pas sûre. Quentin cache quelque chose. Elle en est certaine.

Quentin est assis dans sa voiture. Il ouvre son ordinateur portable. Il cherche des annonces pour des voitures d'occasion. Il y a des voitures bon marché et des voitures chères. Il est **plein d'espoir**. Il cherche une voiture qui serait une bonne affaire. Il a un peu d'argent. Lui et Rashel font des économies. Ils les utilisent pour les vacances. Cette année, Quentin veut une voiture, pas des vacances.

Il voit une annonce pour une vieille voiture. La voiture date de 1990. La voiture est une Jeep. Le modèle est un Grand Wagoneer. Il est **curieux** et veut en savoir plus au sujet de la voiture. Aucune voiture ne ressemble à cette voiture. Il y a du bois à l'extérieur. Quentin pense que c'est cool.

Quentin appelle le numéro de l'annonce.

« Bonjour, dit un homme.

- Bonjour, dit Quentin. J'appelle pour la voiture.

- Quelle voiture ? demande l'homme.

- La Jeep, dit Quentin. Je vais la prendre.

- D'accord, dit l'homme.

- Je viendrai la chercher demain, dit Quentin.

- D'accord! » dit l'homme. Il raccroche le téléphone.

Quentin retourne à la maison. Il se sent **coupable**. Le dîner est froid. Il le mange quand même. Il est **nerveux**. Qu'est-ce que Rashel va penser de la voiture?

Le lendemain, Quentin achète la voiture. Quentin adore la nouvelle voiture. Sa voiture est une Jeep Grand Wagoneer 1990. C'est une grosse voiture. Il y a des panneaux de bois sur le côté.

Quentin rentre à la maison en voiture. La voiture a 120 000 kilomètres au compteur. Elle a environ 30 ans. La voiture est en très bon état. Tout fonctionne. L'intérieur est comme neuf. La nouvelle voiture de Quentin est spéciale. Il n'a pas **honte** de la conduire. Au contraire, il est **fier** de conduire en ville. Que ne pourrait-il pas aimer ?

Il frappe à la porte. Rashel ouvre.

« Rashel, dit-il. Regarde! Quentin pointe du doigt la voiture.

- Tu as une nouvelle voiture ? demande-t-elle.

- Oui, » dit Quentin. Il invite Rashel à monter. Les deux font le tour de la ville. Quentin roule lentement. Beaucoup de gens regardent la voiture. C'est une voiture spéciale. Plusieurs hommes ont l'air **envieux**. Ils veulent une voiture cool. Quentin est enfin **heureux**.

Quentin passe ses journées avec la Jeep. Il la conduit. Parfois, il n'a nulle part où aller. Il ne fait que rouler en ville. Il adore la voiture. Il est **sûr de lui** dans la Jeep. Il passe tous les soirs à nettoyer la voiture. Il astique les portes et les fenêtres tous les soirs. Rashel l'attend. Il est en retard pour le dîner. Cela rend Rashel **furieuse**. Elle déteste la Jeep Wagoneer. Elle pense que Quentin aime la voiture plus qu'il ne l'aime elle. Elle le dit à Quentin et il lui dit de ne pas être **stupide**. Il lui fait un câlin **affectueux**. Il veut lui montrer qu'elle a tort.

Samedi, Rashel et Quentin vont au supermarché. Quentin les conduit en voiture. Les fenêtres sont baissées. Quentin porte des lunettes de soleil. Il semble **confiant** et sûr de lui. Il gare la voiture. Tous les deux vont au supermarché.

Ils achètent des fruits.

« Quentin, peux-tu prendre quatre pommes ? » demande Rashel. Quentin va chercher les fruits. Il revient. Mais il tient quatre oranges.

« Quentin, j'ai dit des pommes! dit Rashel.

- Oui, je sais, dit Quentin.

- Ce sont des oranges! dit Rashel.

- Oh, désolé, dit Quentin. Il est **distrait** et il ne peut pas se concentrer.

- Qu'est-ce qui ne va pas? demande Rashel.

- Rien, dit Quentin.

- À quoi penses-tu? demande-t-elle.

- A rien, dit Quentin. Il a un regard **anxieux**. Il a l'air **inquiet.**

- Penses-tu à la voiture? demande Rashel.

- Non, dit Quentin.

- Oui, tu y penses! Je le sais! Va me chercher des pommes », dit Rashel. Elle **veut vraiment** que Quentin fasse attention. Quentin ramène les pommes. Il les met dans le chariot. Ils finissent leurs courses. Quentin est tranquille. Il a l'air **renfermé**. Ils vont à la voiture.

Le parking est plein. Quentin inspecte soigneusement la jeep. Il a **peur** des marques ou des rayures. Une porte de voiture laisse des marques lorsqu'elle heurte une autre porte. Il y a beaucoup de voitures maintenant. Il ne voit pas de rayures. Quentin déverrouille la voiture. Il monte dans la voiture.

Rashel met les courses dans la voiture. Elle ramène le chariot dans le magasin. Elle ouvre la porte et monte dans la voiture.

« Quentin, je suis **malheureuse**, dit-elle. Elle pleure.

- Quoi? dit Quentin ; il est **surpris**. Qu'est-ce qui ne va pas?

- Tu ne te soucies que de la voiture, dit Rashel.

- Ce n'est pas vrai, affirme Quentin.

- Tu ne m'aides jamais pour rien, dit Rashel.

- Si! Je tiens à toi, dit Quentin.

- Si tu tiens à moi, vends cette voiture, dit Rashel.

RÉSUMÉ

Quentin veut une nouvelle voiture. Il cache ses recherches de voiture à sa petite amie Rashel. Elle lui demande qui appelle. Elle lui demande ce qu'il regarde. Mais Quentin garde ses recherches secrètes. Quentin trouve une voiture qu'il aime. Il est enfin heureux. Cependant, il est trop obsédé par la voiture. Rashel devient jalouse. Quentin ne peut pas se concentrer dans le supermarché. Il craint que quelqu'un n'égratigne la voiture. Quentin n'aide pas Rashel à faire les courses. Elle se met en colère. Elle dit à Quentin qu'il doit choisir entre elle et la voiture.

Liste de Vocabulaire

interested	intéressé
bored	qui s'ennuie
amused	amusé
suspicious	Méfiant

embarrassed	embarrassé
jealous	jaloux
angry	en colère
sad	triste
hopeful	plein d'espoir
curious	curieux
guilty	coupable
nervous	nerveux
ashamed	honteux
proud	fier
envious	envieux
happy	heureux
enraged	furieux
stupid	stupide
loving	affectueux
confident	confiant

distracted	distrait
anxious	anxieux
worried	inquiet
determined	déterminé
withdrawn	renfermé
miserable	misérable
surprised	surpris

QUESTIONS

1) Que pense Quentin de sa voiture au début de l'histoire ?

    a) il l'aime

    b) elle le gêne

    c) elle est trop neuve

    d) elle est trop chère

2) Pourquoi Rashel se fâche-t-il au dîner?

a) elle pense qu'une fille appelle Quentin

b) elle a faim

c) Quentin est en retard

d) Quentin a oublié d'acheter du pain

3) Que fait Quentin au supermarché?

a) il paie pour tout

b) il prend des oranges au lieu des pommes

c) il renverse du lait

d) il fait attention à Rashel

4) Que pense Quentin de sa nouvelle voiture ?

a) elle est trop neuve

b) elle est trop petite

c) il en est fier

d) elle le gêne

5) À la fin de l'histoire, Quentin et Rashel :

    a) s'embrassent

    b) se réconcilient

    c) quittent le magasin

    d) se disputent

RÉPONSES

1) Que pense Quentin de sa voiture au début de l'histoire ?

    b) elle le gêne

2) Pourquoi Rashel se fâche-t-il au dîner?

    a) elle pense qu'une fille appelle Quentin

3) Que fait Quentin à l'épicerie?

    b) il prend des oranges au lieu des pommes

4) Que pense Quentin de sa nouvelle voiture ?

    c) il en est fier

5) À la fin de l'histoire, Quentin et Rashel :

   d) se disputent

Translation of the Story

The Car

STORY

Quentin is **interested** in cars. He looks at pictures of cars. He reads about cars all night, every night. When he is **bored**, he scrolls through Instagram. The accounts he follows are all about cars.

Quentin's girlfriend is Rashel. Rashel is **amused** by Quentin's obsession. Cars do not interest her.

Quentin has a car. Quentin drives a 2000 Honda Accord. His car is green. Quentin feels **embarrassed** by his car. He wants a cool car. He wants a car to drive around town with Rashel. He dreams of nice cars, expensive cars. He wants a big car. Small cars are boring.

Lately, Quentin looks at his phone all the time. When Rashel looks at it, Quentin hides the phone.

"Quentin, why do you hide the phone from me?" asks Rashel.

"No reason," says Quentin.

"That's not true!" says Rashel.

"I promise it is!" says Quentin.

"Then let me see the screen," says Rashel.

"It's nothing," says Quentin. "Forget about it."

Rashel is **suspicious**. Quentin is hiding something.

One night, Rashel makes dinner. Quentin's phone rings. She does not know the number. Quentin answers the phone.

"Hello? Oh. I will call you later," says Quentin. He hangs up.

"Who is it?" says Rashel.

"Nobody," says Quentin.

"Is it a girl?" asks Rashel. She is **jealous**.

"No it is not," says Quentin.

"Then who is it?" asks Rashel.

"Nobody," says Quentin.

"Why won't you tell me?" asks Rashel.

He is so **angry**; Quentin walks out of the house. He leaves the food on the table. It gets cold. Rashel is **sad**. The dinner is a waste. Rashel calls her friend. They talk about the dinner. Rashel's friend thinks Quentin is with another girl. Rashel is unsure. Quentin is hiding something. She is sure.

Quentin sits in his car. He opens his laptop. He searches adverts for second-hand cars. There are cheap cars and expensive cars. He is **hopeful**. He looks for a car that is a good bargain. He has a little money. He and Rashel save money. They use it for vacation. This year, Quentin wants a car, not a vacation.

He sees an advert about an old car. The car is from the year 1990. The car is a Jeep. The model is a Grand Wagoneer. He is **curious** about the car. No cars look like this car. It has wood on the outside. Quentin thinks that is cool.

Quentin calls the number on the advert.

"Hello," says a man.

"Hello," says Quentin. "I am calling about the car."

"Which car?" asks the man.

"The Jeep," says Quentin. "I'll take it."

"Ok," says the man.

"I'll come get it tomorrow," says Quentin.

"Ok!" says the man. He hangs up the phone.

Quentin goes back to the house. He feels **guilty**. Dinner is cold. He eats it anyway. He is **nervous**. What will Rashel think about the car?

The next day, Quentin gets the car. Quentin loves the new car. His car is a 1990 Jeep Grand Wagoneer. It is a big car. It has wood panels along the side.

Quentin drives to the house. The car has 120,000 kilometers. It is about 30 years old. The car is in very good condition. Everything works. The interior is like new. Quentin's new car is special. He does not feel **ashamed** driving. On the contrary, he feels **proud** driving through town. What is not to love?

He knocks on the door. Rashel opens it.

"Rashel," he says. "Look!" Quentin points at the car.

"You have a new car?" she asks.

"Yes," says Quentin. He invites Rashel to ride. The two drive around town. Quentin drives slow. Many people stare at the car. It is a special car.

Several men look **envious**. They want a cool car. Quentin is finally **happy**.

Quentin spends every day with the Jeep. He drives it. Sometimes he has nowhere to go. He just drives around town. He loves the car. He feels **confident** in the Jeep. He spends every evening cleaning the car. He polishes the doors and windows every night. Rashel waits for him. He is late for dinner. This makes Rashel **enraged**. She hates the Jeep Wagoneer. She thinks Quentin loves the car more than he loves her. She tells Quentin this and he tells her not to be **stupid**. He gives her a **loving** hug. He wants to show her she is wrong.

On Saturday, Rashel and Quentin go to the supermarket. Quentin drives them. The windows are down. Quentin wears sunglasses. He looks **confident** and sure of himself. He parks the car. The two go into the supermarket.

They shop for fruit.

"Quentin, can you get four apples?" asks Rashel. Quentin goes to get the fruit. He returns. But he has four oranges.

"Quentin, I said apples!" says Rashel.

"Yeah, I know," says Quentin.

"These are oranges!" says Rashel.

"Oh, sorry," says Quentin. He is **distracted**. He cannot concentrate.

"What is wrong?" asks Rashel.

"Nothing," says Quentin.

"What are you thinking about?" she asks.

"Nothing," says Quentin. He has an **anxious** look. He has a **worried** look in his eyes.

"Are you thinking about the car?" asks Rashel.

"No," says Quentin.

"Yes you are! I know it! Go get me some apples," says Rashel. She is **determined** to make Quentin pay attention. Quentin brings back the apples. He puts them in the cart. They finish grocery shopping. Quentin is quiet. He seems **withdrawn**. They go to the car.

The parking lot is full. Quentin inspects the Jeep carefully. He is **afraid** of marks or scratches. A car door leaves marks when it hits another door. There are many cars now. He does not see any scratches. Quentin unlocks the car. He gets in.

Rashel puts the groceries in the car. She returns the cart to the store. She opens the door and gets in.

"Quentin, I am **miserable**," she says. She is crying.

"What?" says Quentin. He is **surprised**. What is wrong?

"You only care about the car," says Rashel.

"That's not true," says Quentin.

"You don't help me do anything," says Rashel.

"I do! I care about you," says Quentin.

"If you care about me, sell this car," says Rashel.

CHAPTER 2
Going to A Meeting / telling time

HISTOIRE

Thomas quitte son appartement. C'est une belle journée. Le soleil brille. L'air est frais. Thomas a une réunion importante aujourd'hui. Thomas est le PDG d'une entreprise. Aujourd'hui, il rencontre de nouveaux investisseurs. Il est prêt pour la réunion. Il est détendu.

Il est **huit heures du matin**. Thomas marche dans la rue. Il est en avance. Il veut **plus de temps**. Il ne veut pas être en retard. Il ne veut pas être stressé.

Thomas vit dans une grande ville. Il y a de grands immeubles partout. Les taxis passent. Beaucoup de voitures passent. Thomas aime marcher. Parfois, il prend le métro.

Thomas veut prendre son petit-déjeuner. Il s'arrête à un café. L'atmosphère du café est détendue. Il y a de la musique. Thomas veut une pâtisserie.

« Que désirez-vous ? demande le barista.

- Un muffin, s'il vous plaît, dit Thomas.

- Myrtille ou chocolat ? demande le barista.

- Myrtille, s'il vous plaît, dit Thomas.

- Quelque chose à boire ? demande le barista.

- Un café, dit Thomas.

- Un café noir ? demande le barista.

- Non, avec un peu de crème, dit-il.

- À emporter? demande le barista. Thomas regarde sa montre. Il est **huit heures et demie**. Il a le temps.

« Pour ici », dit Thomas. Il s'assoit et mange. Il regarde les gens passer. Thomas regarde encore sa montre. Il est neuf heures **pile**. Il se lève. Thomas jette les déchets et aux toilettes. Il enlève sa montre pour se laver les mains. Sa montre est en or et il n'aime pas la mouiller. Son téléphone sonne.

« Bonjour, dit Thomas.

- Monsieur, êtes-vous au bureau? demande la secrétaire de Thomas.

- Pas encore, dit Thomas. Je suis en route. »

Il quitte le café. Thomas marche vers le métro. Il a le temps, alors il n'a pas besoin de prendre un taxi. Il regarde à nouveau sa montre. Mais sa montre n'est pas là. Thomas panique. Il repense à sa matinée. Est-ce qu'il l'a laissée à la maison? Non. Il se rappelle avoir enlevé la montre et s'être lavé les mains. La montre est au café.

Thomas retourne au café.

« Excusez-moi, avez-vous une montre en or? demande-t-il.

- Un instant, dit le barista. Il demande à ses collègues. Personne n'a la montre.

- Non, » dit le barista. Thomas va aux toilettes. Il regarde près de l'évier. La montre n'est pas là. Quelqu'un a la montre, pense Thomas. Il n'a plus le temps de la chercher.

« Excusez-moi, dit-il encore au barista, quelle heure est-il ?

- **Il est dix oh, non neuf heures** », dit le barista.

- Merci, dit Thomas. Thomas se dépêche. La réunion est à 11 h 45. Il se précipite vers l'arrêt de métro. Il y a une longue file d'attente pour acheter des billets. Il attend cinq **minutes**.

« Avez-vous l'heure? demande Thomas à une femme.

- Il dix heures **trente** », dit-elle. Thomas est en retard. Il quitte la longue file d'attente. Il se rend dans la rue. Il appelle un taxi. Tous les taxis sont pleins. Enfin, un taxi s'arrête. Thomas monte dans le taxi.

« Où allez-vous? demande le chauffeur.

- Entre la 116e et le Parc, dit Thomas.

- D'accord, dit le chauffeur.

- Dépêchez-vous, dit Thomas. Je dois être **à l'heure** pour une réunion.

- Oui, monsieur », dit le chauffeur.

Thomas arrive au bureau. Il sort en courant du taxi et monte les escaliers. Sa secrétaire lui dit bonjour. Thomas est en sueur!

« Monsieur, la réunion est maintenant **dans une heure** », dit la secrétaire. Thomas essuie la sueur de son visage.

« Bien », dit Thomas. Il se prépare pour la réunion. Sa chemise est mouillée. Elle sent mauvais. Thomas décide d'acheter une nouvelle chemise pour la réunion.

Thomas va au magasin en bas de la rue.

« Bonjour, monsieur, dit le vendeur. Comment pouvons-nous vous aider?

- J'ai besoin d'une nouvelle chemise », dit Thomas. Le vendeur emmène Thomas voir les chemises. Il y a des chemises roses, des chemises brunes, des chemises à carreaux et des chemises à motif écossais. Le vendeur parle beaucoup. Thomas est nerveux au sujet de l'heure.

« **Quelle heure est-il**? demande Thomas au vendeur.

- Il est **presque midi**, dit le vendeur.

- D'accord, dit Thomas. Donnez-moi la chemise brune. » La vendeuse apporte la chemise brune à la caisse. Elle plie la chemise. **Elle prend son temps**.

Le téléphone de Thomas sonne. C'est sa femme.

« Chéri, nous dînons à **19 heures**, dit-elle.

- Ok, chérie, dit Thomas. Je ne peux pas vraiment parler maintenant.

- D'accord, dit-elle. Je ne veux juste pas que tu rentres à la maison à neuf heures **du soir**.

- Ne t'inquiète pas, dit Thomas.

- Au revoir », dit sa femme. Thomas raccroche le téléphone.

« Excusez-moi, dit Thomas. Je suis pressé. Je n'ai pas besoin que la chemise soit emballée.

- D'accord », dit-elle. Thomas paie et quitte le magasin. Il change de chemise en marchant dans la rue. Les gens le regardent. Il se précipite au bureau.

« **Il est grand temps** », dit sa secrétaire lorsqu'il arrive. Ils attendent dans la salle de réunion. Les investisseurs sont assis autour de la table. Thomas dit bonjour.

« J'aime votre chemise, Thomas, dit l'un des investisseurs.

- Merci, dit Thomas. Elle est nouvelle. » Thomas pose son téléphone et allume son ordinateur.

« Merci d'être venus, dit Thomas. J'ai une présentation. Elle dure environ quinze minutes. »

Thomas se tourne vers sa secrétaire. « Quelle heure est-il? »

« Il est **midi heures quinze**, dit-elle.

- Merci, dit Thomas. Ma montre a disparu. »

« Pourquoi ne regardez-vous pas votre téléphone pour avoir l'heure? dit l'un des investisseurs.

- Bien sûr », dit Thomas. Il est tellement habitué à sa montre qu'il oublie qu'il peut regarder l'heure sur son téléphone!

« Je dois être la dernière personne au monde à n'utiliser qu'une montre pour **avoir l'heure** », dit Thomas. Tout le monde rit.

RÉSUMÉ

Thomas commence sa journée en avance. Il prend son petit déjeuner et se détend. Il va aux toilettes et laisse sa montre dans les toilettes. Quand il s'en rend compte, il retourne au café. La montre a disparu. Maintenant, il doit demander à tout le monde quelle heure il est. Il arrive au bureau en retard. Heureusement, sa réunion est reportée d'une heure. Il va acheter une nouvelle chemise. Cela prend plus de temps que prévu. Il se précipite à sa réunion. Lorsqu'il demande l'heure, encore une fois, il se rend compte qu'il pourrait simplement regarder son téléphone pour avoir l'heure. La réunion commence.

Liste de Vocabulaire

It is ___ o'clock	Il est ___ heures
in the morning	le matin
time	temps
half past ___	___ et demie
on the dot	exactement
second	seconde

www.LearnLikeNatives.com

What time is it?	Quelle heure est-il ?
___ oh ___	___ oh ___
a.m.	10 h 30.
a quarter to ___	___ et quart
minutes	minutes
Do you have the time?	Vous avez l'heure?
___ thirty	___ trente
on time	à l'heure
in an hour	dans une heure
What's the time?	Quelle heure est-il ?
nearly	presque
noon	midi
takes her time	prend son temps
p.m.	dans l'après-midi
at night	la nuit
about time	il est temps

____ minutes long	____ minutes
____ fifteen	____ quinze
tell the time	dire l'heure

QUESTIONS

1) Pourquoi Thomas perd-il sa montre ?

    a) Elle tombe

    b) Il laisse un étranger la prendre

    c) Il fait un pari

    d) Il l'enlève pour se laver les mains

2) Où vit Thomas?

    a) dans une petite ville

    b) dans une ville avec peu de moyens de transport

    c) dans une grande ville

    d) à la campagne

3) Thomas est chanceux parce que :

    a) il a de bons collègues

    b) sa réunion est reportée

    c) le métro n'est pas bondé

    d) il ne perd pas sa montre

4) Thomas dit au vendeur de ne pas emballer la chemise parce que :

    a) il est en retard pour sa réunion

    b) il y a de la sueur sur sa chemise

    c) sa femme attend au téléphone

    d) il déteste gaspiller des sacs

5) Tout le monde rit à la fin de l'histoire parce que :

    a) La chemise de Thomas est pleine de sueur

b) Thomas est gêné

c) Thomas oublie que l'on peut lire l'heure sur son téléphone

d) Thomas perd sa montre.

RÉPONSES

1) Pourquoi Thomas perd-il sa montre ?

d) Il l'enlève pour se laver les mains

2) Où vit Thomas?

c) dans une grande ville

3) Thomas est chanceux parce que :

b) sa réunion est reportée

4) Thomas dit au vendeur de ne pas emballer la chemise parce que :

a) il est en retard pour sa réunion

5) Tout le monde rit à la fin de l'histoire parce que :

c) Thomas oublie que l'on peut lire l'heure sur son téléphone

www.LearnLikeNatives.com

Translation of the Story

Going to A Meeting

STORY

Thomas leaves his apartment building. It is a beautiful day. The sun shines. The air is fresh. Thomas has an important meeting today. Thomas is the CEO of a company. Today he meets with new investors. He is prepared for the meeting. He feels relaxed.

It is **eight o'clock in the morning**. Thomas walks down the city street. He is early. He wants extra **time**. He does not want to be late. He does not want to stress.

Thomas lives in a big city. There are tall buildings everywhere. Taxis drive by. Lots of cars drive by.

Thomas likes to walk. Sometimes he takes the subway.

Thomas wants to eat breakfast. He stops at a café. The café is relaxed. Music plays. Thomas wants a baked good.

"What would you like?" asks the barista.

"A muffin please," says Thomas.

"Blueberry or chocolate?" asks the barista.

"Blueberry, please," says Thomas.

"Anything to drink?" asks the barista.

"A coffee," says Thomas.

"Black?" asks the barista.

"No, with a bit of cream," he says.

"To go?" asks the barista. Thomas looks at his watch. It is **half past eight.** He has time.

"For here," says Thomas. He sits down and eats. He watches people walk by. Thomas looks at his watch again. It is nine o'clock **on the dot**. He gets up. Thomas throws out the trash and goes to the bathroom. He takes off his watch to wash his hands. His watch is gold and he doesn't like to get it wet. His phone rings.

"Hello," says Thomas.

"Sir, are you at the office?" asks Thomas's secretary.

"Not yet," says Thomas. "I'm on my way."

He leaves the coffee shop. Thomas walks towards the subway. He has time, so he doesn't need a taxi. He looks at his watch again. But his watch is not there. Thomas feels panic. He thinks back over the morning. Did he leave it at home? No. He remembers taking off the watch and washing his hands. The watch is at the coffee shop.

Thomas runs back to the coffee shop.

"Excuse me," he says to the barista.

"Do you have a gold watch?" he asks.

"Just a **second**," says the barista. He asks his colleagues. No one has the watch.

"No," says the barista. Thomas goes to the bathroom. He looks by the sink. The watch is not there. Someone has the watch, Thomas thinks. He has no time to look any more.

"Excuse me," he says to the barista again.

"**What time is it?**" he asks.

"**Ten oh nine a.m.**" says the barista.

"Thanks," says Thomas. Thomas hurries. He has the meeting at a quarter to eleven. He rushes to the subway stop. There is a long line to buy tickets. He waits for five **minutes**.

"Do you have the time?" Thomas asks a woman.

"It's ten **thirty**," she says. Thomas is late. He leave the long line. He goes to the street. He waves for a taxi. All the taxis are full. Finally, a taxi stops. Thomas gets into the taxi.

"Where are you going?" asks the driver.

"To 116th and Park," says Thomas.

"Ok," says the driver.

"Please hurry," says Thomas. "I need to be **on time** for a meeting."

"Yes, sir," says the driver.

Thomas arrives to the office. He runs out of the taxi and up the stairs. His secretary says hello. Thomas is sweaty!

"Sir, the meeting is now **in an hour**," says the secretary. Thomas wipes the sweat off his face.

"Good," says Thomas. He prepares for the meeting. His shirt is sweaty. It smells bad. Thomas decides to buy a new shirt for the meeting.

Thomas goes to the store down the street.

"Hi, sir," says the salesperson. "How can we help you?"

"I need a new dress shirt," says Thomas. The salesperson takes Thomas to see the shirts. There are pink shirts, brown shirts, checked shirts, and plaid shirts. The salesperson talks a lot. Thomas is nervous about the time.

"**What's the time?**" Thomas asks the salesperson.

"It's **nearly noon**," says the salesperson.

"Ok," says Thomas. "Give me the brown shirt." The salesperson takes the brown shirt to the cash register. She folds the shirt. She **takes her time**.

Thomas's phone rings. It is his wife.

"Honey, we have dinner at seven **p.m.**," she says.

"Ok, dear," says Thomas. "I can't really talk right now."

"Ok," she says. "I just don't want you to come home at nine o'clock **at night**."

"Don't worry," says Thomas.

"Bye," says his wife. Thomas hangs up the phone.

"Excuse me," says Thomas. "I'm in a hurry. I don't need the shirt wrapped."

"Ok," she says. Thomas pays and leaves the store. He changes his shirt as he walks down the street. People stare. He hurries to the office.

"It's **about time**," says his secretary when he walks in. They are waiting in the meeting. The investors sit around the table. Thomas says hello.

"I like your shirt, Thomas," says one of the investors.

"Thanks," says Thomas. "It is new." Thomas sets his phone down and turns on his computer.

"Thank you for coming," says Thomas. "I have a presentation. It is about fifteen minutes long."

Thomas turns to his secretary. "What time is it?"

"It is **twelve fifteen**," she says.

"Thanks," says Thomas. "My watch is missing."

"Why don't you look at your phone for the time?" says one of the investors.

"Of course," says Thomas. He is so accustomed to his watch that he forgets he can look at the phone for the time!

"I must be the last person in the world to only use a watch to **tell the time**," says Thomas. Everyone laughs.

CHAPTER 3
Lunch with The Queen / to be, to have + food

HISTOIRE

Ursula **est** une jeune fille. Elle vit à Londres, en Angleterre. Elle étudie à l'école. Elle aime cuisiner. Elle **a** une obsession : la famille royale. Elle veut **être** une princesse.

Un soir, Ursula est à la maison. Sa mère prépare son dîner. Elles **ont** quelque chose de nouveau. Sa mère apporte l'assiette sur la table.

« Qu'est-ce que c'**est** ? demande Ursula.

- Ce sont des **poireaux**, dit la mère d'Ursula.

- Oh, je n'aime pas les poireaux, dit Ursula.

- Essaie, dit sa mère. Elle essaie. Elle vomit presque.

« Je **suis** malade, dit Ursula.

- Non, tu ne l'es pas, dit sa mère.

- S'il te plaît, donne-moi d'autres **légumes**, dit Ursula, **carottes, brocoli, salade**? »

- Oh, Ursula, mange ta **viande** alors, dit sa mère. Elle allume la télévision. Elles regardent les infos. Le reportage parle de la Reine d'Angleterre.

Ursula arrête de manger. Elle écoute attentivement.

« La reine Elizabeth règne en Angleterre depuis 68 ans, dit le journal. Elle est mariée au prince Phillip. Ils ont quatre enfants. »

Le reportage parle de la Reine. Elle vit à Buckingham Palace. Elle est en très bonne santé, malgré son âge.

« Je veux visiter le palais de Buckingham, dit Ursula.

- Oui, ma chérie, dit sa mère. Elles regardent l'émission. L'émission annonce un concours spécial. Une personne peut gagner une visite au palais de Buckingham. Le gagnant **déjeunera** avec la reine. Ursula hurle.

« Je **dois** gagner! crie-t-elle.

- Je ne sais pas, dit sa mère, beaucoup de gens participent au concours. »

Ursula regarde le programme. Elle découvre comment participer. Elle prend une photo d'elle en train de manger. Ensuite, elle l'affiche sur les médias sociaux. Elle regarde le programme, qui parle de manger avec la reine. Elle regarde ce qui est arrivé à un prince du Pacifique Sud.

La reine est sur un bateau avec le prince. On sert le **dessert**. Le prince oublie de regarder la reine. Il prend des **raisins** et des **cerises** parmi les **fruits** sur la table et les met dans son bol. Il verse de la **crème** sur eux. Il saupoudre du **sucre** sur le dessus. Il commence à manger, puis il se rend compte que la Reine ne l'a pas fait. Il fait une grosse erreur. La Reine prend sa cuillère. Elle mange un peu. Le prince se sent mieux. Il est très gêné.

« Il y a des règles pour manger avec la Reine? demande-t-elle à sa mère.

- Bien sûr, dit sa mère.

- Comme quoi ? demande Ursula.

- Eh bien, la reine commence le **repas** et le termine, dit la mère d'Ursula.

- Tu veux dire qu'on ne peut pas manger jusqu'à ce qu'elle le fasse, dit Ursula.

- C'est exact, dit sa mère. Et quand elle a fini, tu finis aussi.

- Et si on n'a pas terminé ? demande Ursula.

- On a terminé, dit sa mère. Et on doit attendre que la Reine s'assoie.

- Avant de s'asseoir ? dit Ursula.

- C'est ça, dit sa mère. Ursula y pense. Il y a beaucoup de règles si vous êtes reine ou princesse. Ursula et sa mère terminent le dîner. Elles vont se coucher.

Le lendemain matin, Ursula se réveille. Elle est nerveuse au sujet du concours. Aujourd'hui, on annonce le gagnant. Elle prend le **petit-déjeuner** avec sa mère.

« Je suis nerveuse, dit-elle.

- Ursula, tu ne gagneras pas, dit sa mère. Tant de gens participent au concours.

- Oh » dit Ursula. Elle est triste. Elle mange ses **céréales**. Elle n'a pas faim. Elle ne touche pas à son **bacon** et ses **œufs**.

Elles allument la télévision.

« Et nous annonçons le gagnant du concours pour le déjeuner avec la Reine », explique l'homme à la télévision. Il met sa main dans un énorme bol en verre rempli de papiers. Il secoue la main. Il sort un papier. Il ouvre le papier.

« Et la gagnante est... Ursula Vann ! », dit-il.

Ursula regarde sa mère. Sa mère la regarde.

« As-tu entendu cela? demande-t-elle. Sa mère hoche la tête, le regard fixe. Sa bouche est ouverte.

- Ai-je gagné? demande-t-elle. Sa mère acquiesce, sans voix.

- Youhou! s'écrie Ursula. Je savais que j'y arriverai! Je vais voir la Reine! » Ursula termine son plat et va à l'école.

Le lendemain, c'est le jour du déjeuner avec la Reine. Ursula se dirige vers le palais. Elle est terrifiée. Elle n'est qu'une jeune fille. C'est une grande aventure pour une si jeune fille.

« Qui êtes-vous ? demande un gardien.

- Ursula Vann, dit-elle. J'ai gagné le concours pour déjeuner avec la reine.

- Oh, bonjour, jeune fille, dit le gardien. Vous êtes une fille plutôt jeune. Entrez.

- Merci, dit-elle.

Un garde l'emmène au palais. C'est grandiose et très grand. Ils traversent les couloirs. Le garde a un drôle de chapeau. Ursula rit. Puis, elle s'arrête. Ils sont dans la salle à manger.

La Reine d'Angleterre est assise à la table! Il y a une assiette de **sandwichs** devant elle. Elle est petite. Elle est heureuse, et elle sourit.

« Bonjour, ma chère, dit-elle.

- Bonjour, Votre Majesté, dit Ursula. Elle fait la révérence.

- Merci d'être venue déjeuner, dit-elle.

www.LearnLikeNatives.com

- C'est un plaisir, Votre **Majesté**, dit Ursula.

- J'espère que cela ne vous dérange pas. Nous prendrons le **thé** au lieu d'un bon repas », dit la reine. Elle s'assoit de nouveau. Ursula se souvient de ses manières. Elle s'assoit aussi.

« Les sandwichs sont des sandwichs royaux, pense-t-elle. Ils ressemblent beaucoup à des sandwichs de la maison, cependant. Certains ont du **jambon** et du **fromage**, avec un peu de **moutarde** jaune. D'autres sont tartinés de salade de **mayonnaise**. Il y a une assiette de **biscuits** à côté de quelques **scones**.

« Pardonnez-moi, Votre Majesté, dit Ursula.

- Oui, ma chère ? dit la reine.

- Qu'y a-t-il sur ce sandwich ? demande-t-elle.

- Oh, c'est mon plat préféré, dit la reine. Sandwich à la **salade** de poireaux.

- Oh, les poireaux, dit Ursula. Elle se sent malade. La Reine lui en tend un. Elle en prend une bouchée.

- Prenez-en un, ma chère, dit la reine.

- Merci, Votre Majesté, dit Ursula. Elle prend un sandwich aux poireaux. Elle peut sentir son estomac se retourner. Elle prend une bouchée énorme parce qu'elle est très nerveuse. Son visage devient blanc, puis vert.

« Ça va, ma chère ? demande la Reine. Vous avez l'air très malade.

- Je vais bien », dit Ursula. Elle sent son estomac se retourner. Elle a l'impression qu'elle va vomir. Elle ne peut pas empêcher les poireaux de remonter dans sa gorge. Au moins elle a suivi les autres règles pour manger avec la Reine, pense-t-elle. Personne n'a jamais parlé de vomir.

RÉSUMÉ

Ursula est une jeune fille. Elle vit à Londres, en Angleterre. Elle est obsédée par la famille royale. Elle dîne avec sa mère et regarde la télévision. À la télévision, ils annoncent un concours. Le gagnant peut déjeuner avec la reine elle-même. Ursula entre. Le lendemain, au petit déjeuner, ils annoncent le gagnant. C'est Ursula ! Elle se rend au Palais de Buckingham pour le déjeuner. Elle suit les règles pour manger avec la Reine. La Reine a préparé des sandwichs spéciaux. Malheureusement, la salade de poireaux n'est pas le plat préféré d'Ursula. Elle se sent malade quand elle regarde la reine manger le sandwich.

is	est
has	a
to be	être
have	avoir
are	sont
leeks	poireaux
am	suis
vegetable	légumes
carrot	carotte
broccoli	brocoli
salad	salade
lunch	déjeuner
have to	devoir
dessert	dessert
grapes	raisins
cherries	cerises

fruit	fruit
cream	crème
sugar	sucre
meal	repas
breakfast	petit déjeuner
cereal	céréales
egg	œuf
bacon	bacon
sandwiches	sandwichs
tea	thé
ham	jambon
cheese	fromage
mustard	moutarde
cookies	cookies
scones	scones
salad	salade

QUESTIONS

1) Que se passe-t-il lorsqu'Ursula essaie les poireaux pour la première fois?

    a) elle les aime

    b) sa mère les brûle

    c) elle a presque vomi

    d) elle ne les remarque pas

2) Quelle est la règle pour manger avec la reine d'Angleterre?

    a) vous ne devez pas manger avant elle

    b) vous devez porter du bleu

    c) vous devez manger des sandwichs

    d) vous devez vous asseoir avant elle

3) Que pense la mère d'Ursula du concours?

    a) Ursula a une chance de gagner

b) c'est un faux concours

c) la Reine ne devrait pas participer

d) Ursula ne gagnera jamais

4) Qu'est-ce que la reine a à manger?

a) un bon rôti

b) du saumon, son préféré

c) des biscuits et sandwichs

d) c'est top secret

.

5) Lequel des énoncés suivants est vrai?

a) Ursula part en plein milieu du déjeuner

b) Ursula ne peut pas contrôler sa réaction face aux poireaux

c) la Reine a fait les sandwichs elle-même

d) les sandwichs ne sont pas bons pour le déjeuner

RÉPONSES

1) Que se passe-t-il lorsque Ursula essaie les poireaux pour la première fois?

c) elle a presque vomi

2) Quelle est la règle lorsque vous mangez avec la Reine d'Angleterre?

a) vous ne devez pas manger avant elle

3) Que pense la mère d'Ursula du concours?

d) Ursula ne gagnera jamais

4) Qu'est-ce que la reine a à manger?

c) biscuits et sandwichs

5) Lequel des énoncés suivants est vrai?

b) Ursula ne peut pas contrôler sa réaction face aux poireaux

Translation of the Story

Lunch with The Queen

STORY

Ursula **is** a young girl. She lives in London, England. She studies at school. She loves to bake. She **has** an obsession: the royal family. She wants **to be** a princess.

One night, Ursula is at home. Her mother prepares her dinner. They **have** something new. Her mother brings the plate to the table.

"What **are** those?" asks Ursula.

"These are **leeks**," says Ursula's mom.

"Oh, I don't like leeks," says Ursula.

"Try them," says her mom. She tries them. She almost vomits.

"I **am** sick," says Ursula.

"No, you are not," says her mom.

"Please, give me any other **vegetable**," says Ursula. "**Carrots**, **broccoli**, **salad**?"

"Oh, Ursula, just eat your **meat** then," says her mom. She turns on the television. They watch the news. The report is about the Queen of England. Ursula stops eating. She pays close attention.

"Queen Elizabeth reigns in England for 68 years," says the news report. "She is married to Prince Phillip. They have four children."

The news report talks about the Queen. She lives in Buckingham Palace. She is very healthy, despite her age.

"I want to visit Buckingham Palace," says Ursula.

"Yes, dear," says her mom. They watch the program. The program announces a special competition. One person can win a visit to Buckingham Palace. The winner will eat **lunch** with the queen. Ursula screams.

"I **have to** win!" she shouts.

"I don't know," says her mom. "Many people enter the contest."

Ursula watches the program. She learns how to enter. She takes a picture of herself eating. Then she posts it on social media. She watches the program, which talks about eating with the Queen. She watches as they show what happened to a prince from the South Pacific.

The Queen is on a boat with the prince. They serve **dessert**. The prince forgets to watch the Queen. He takes some **grapes** and some **cherries** from the **fruit** on the table and puts them in his bowl. He pours **cream** over them. He sprinkles **sugar** on top. He starts to eat, and then he realizes the Queen has not. He makes a big mistake. The Queen takes her spoon. She eats a bit. That makes the prince feel better. He is very embarrassed.

"There are rules to eat with the Queen?" she asks her mom.

"Of course," says her mom.

"Like what?" asks Ursula.

"Well, the Queen begins the **meal** and ends the meal," says Ursula's mom.

"You mean you can't eat until she does," says Ursula.

"That's right," says her mom. "And when she finishes, you finish, too."

"What if you aren't finished?" asks Ursula.

"You are," says her mom. "And you must wait for the Queen to sit."

"Before you sit?" says Ursula.

"Right," says her mom. Ursula thinks about this. There are lots of rules if you are queen or princess. Ursula and her mom finish dinner. They go to sleep.

The next morning, Ursula wakes up. She is nervous about the contest. Today they announce the winner. She eats **breakfast** with her mom.

"I am nervous," she says.

"Ursula, you won't win," says her mom. "So many people are in the contest."

"Oh," says Ursula. She is sad. She eats her **cereal**. She is not hungry. Her **bacon** and **eggs** sit untouched.

They turn on the television.

"And we announce the winner of the Lunch with the Queen Contest," says the man on the TV. He puts his hand into a huge glass bowl full of papers. He moves his hand around. He pulls out a paper. He opens the paper.

"And the winner is…Ursula Vann!" he says.

Ursula looks at her mom. Her mom looks at her.

"Did you hear that?" she asks. Her mom nods, staring. Her mouth is open.

"Did I win?" she asks. Her mom nods, speechless.

"Woo-hoo!" shouts Ursula. "I knew I would! I'm going to see the queen!" Ursula finishes her food and goes to school.

The next day is the day for lunch with the Queen. Ursula walks up to the palace. She is terrified. She is only a young girl. This is a big adventure for such a young girl.

"Who are you?" asks a guard.

"Ursula Vann," she says. "I won the contest to have lunch with the Queen."

"Oh, hello, young lady," the guard says. "You are a pretty young lass. Come in."

"Thank you," she says.

A guard takes her to the palace. It is grand, and very big. They walk through the halls. The guard has a funny hat. Ursula giggles. Then, she stops. They are in the dining room.

The Queen of England is sitting at the table! There is a plate of **sandwiches** in front of her. She is small. She is happy, and she is smiling.

"Hello, dear," she says.

"Hello, your majesty," Ursula says. She courtsies.

"Thank you for coming to lunch," she says.

"It is my pleasure, your **Majesty**," says Ursula.

"I hope you don't mind. We will be having **tea** instead of a proper lunch," says the Queen. She sits again. Ursula remembers her manners. She sits, too.

The sandwiches are royal sandwiches, she thinks. They look a lot like sandwiches from home, though. Some have **ham** and **cheese**, with a yellow bit of **mustard**. Others have a **mayonnaise** salad on them. There is a plate of **cookies** next to some **scones**.

"Pardon me, your Majesty," says Ursula.

"Yes, dear?" says the Queen.

"What is on that sandwich?" she asks.

"Oh, that's my favorite," says the Queen. "Leek **salad** sandwich."

"Oh, leeks," says Ursula. She feels sick. The Queen reaches for one. She takes a bite.

"Have one, dear," says the Queen.

"Thank you, your Majesty," says Ursula. She takes a leek sandwich. She can feel her stomach turn. She takes a huge bite because she is so nervous. Her face turns white, then green.

"Are you alright, dear?" asks the Queen. "You look quite unwell."

"I- I- I'm fine," says Ursula. She feels her stomach turning. She feels as if she will vomit. She can't stop the leeks from coming back up her throat. At least she followed the other rules for eating lunch with the Queen, she thinks. Nobody ever said anything about vomiting.

CONCLUSION

You did it!

You finished a whole book in a brand-new language. That in and of itself is quite the accomplishment, isn't it?

Congratulate yourself on time well spent and a job well done. Now that you've finished the book, you have familiarized yourself with over 500 new vocabulary words, comprehended the heart of 3 short stories, and listened to loads of dialogue unfold, all without going anywhere!

Charlemagne said "To have another language is to possess a second soul." After immersing yourself in this book, you are broadening your horizons and opening a whole new path for yourself.

Have you thought about how much you know now that you did not know before? You've learned everything from how to greet and how to express your emotions to basics like colors and place words. You can tell time and ask question. All without opening a schoolbook. Instead, you've cruised through fun, interesting stories and possibly listened to them as well.

Perhaps before you weren't able to distinguish meaning when you listened to French. If you used the audiobook, we bet you can now pick out meanings and words when you hear someone speaking. Regardless, we are sure you have taken an important step to being more fluent. You are well on your way!

Best of all, you have made the essential step of distinguishing in your mind the idea that most often hinders people studying a new language. By approaching French through our short stories and dialogs, instead of formal lessons with just grammar and vocabulary, you are no longer in the 'learning' mindset. Your approach is much more similar to an osmosis, focused on speaking and using the language, which is the end goal, after all!

So, what's next?

This is just the first of five books, all packed full of short stories and dialogs, covering essential, everyday French that will ensure you master the basics. You can find the rest of the books in the series, as well as a whole host of other resources, at LearnLikeNatives.com. Simply add the book to your library to take the next step in your language learning journey. If you are ever in need of new ideas or direction, refer to our 'Speak Like a Native' eBook, available to you for free at LearnLikeNatives.com, which clearly outlines practical steps you can take to continue learning any language you choose.

www.LearnLikeNatives.com

We also encourage you to get out into the real world and practice your French. You have a leg up on most beginners, after all—instead of pure textbook learning, you have been absorbing the sound and soul of the language. Do not underestimate the foundation you have built reviewing the chapters of this book. Remember, no one feels 100% confident when they speak with a native speaker in another language.

One of the coolest things about being human is connecting with others. Communicating with someone in their own language is a wonderful gift. Knowing the language turns you into a local and opens up your world. You will see the reward of learning languages for many years to come, so keep that practice up!. Don't let your fears stop you from taking the chance to use your French. Just give it a try, and remember that you will make mistakes. However, these mistakes will teach you so much, so view every single one as a small victory! Learning is growth.

www.LearnLikeNatives.com

Don't let the quest for learning end here! There is so much you can do to continue the learning process in an organic way, like you did with this book. Add another book from Learn Like a Native to your library. Listen to French talk radio. Watch some of the great French films. Put on the latest CD from Edith Piaf. Take cooking lessons in French. Whatever you do, don't stop because every little step you take counts towards learning a new language, culture, and way of communicating.

www.LearnLikeNatives.com

www.LearnLikeNatives.com

Learn Like a Native is a revolutionary **language education brand** that is taking the linguistic world by storm. Forget boring grammar books that never get you anywhere, Learn Like a Native teaches you languages in a fast and fun way that actually works!

As an international, multichannel, language learning platform, we provide **books, audio guides and eBooks** so that you can acquire the knowledge you need, swiftly and easily.

Our **subject-based learning**, structured around real-world scenarios, builds your conversational muscle and ensures you learn the content most relevant to your requirements. Discover our tools at ***LearnLikeNatives.com***.

When it comes to learning languages, we've got you covered!

www.ingramcontent.com/pod-product-compliance
Lightning Source LLC
Chambersburg PA
CBHW071743080526
44588CB00013B/2137